YOLANDA ZAPPATERRA
AND SARAH GUY

FREE LONDON

EXPLORE THE CAPITAL WITHOUT BREAKING THE BANK

FRANCES
LINCOLN

CONTENTS

INTRODUCTION

London, contrary to popular misconceptions, is a generous city. There are hundreds of activities and experiences out there, free to both locals and visitors, whatever their ages or interests. Yes, the city can be expensive, but it doesn't have to be. From world-class galleries and museums to sports and entertainment, the capital is filled with things to do for absolutely nothing. Finding the right activity for the right occasion isn't always easy, so to spark the imagination we've gathered together more than a hundred of the very best, some familiar, others less so.

Grouped into seven categories - things to do outdoors; green spaces; museums; galleries; performing arts; buildings and built spaces; and seasonal - our selection includes activities that will delight children, and events that will open up a world of talks, walks, spaces and happenings for older readers. There are suggestions for rainy-day pursuits, as well as options for exploring the great outdoors; chances to connect through group sessions, and places to find calm and solitude or excitement and celebration. You could watch a firework display, marvel at centuries-old pageantry or catch an open-air screening. Parks, city farms, playgrounds, museums, concerts, talks and festivals are all covered, together with some of London's most idiosyncratic attractions and wonderfully alluring oddities. Whichever experience you plump for, *Free London* will connect you with the city in rewarding and sometimes surprising new ways. We hope you have as much fun discovering them as we did!

1

THINGS TO DO OUTDOORS

❧ MUDCHUTE CITY FARM

EAST LONDON

Of the many excellent city farms to be found in London, why have we plumped for Mudchute? It begins with the journey here, on the always enjoyable Docklands Light Railway (DLR), which wends its way through the once mighty, now dwarfed, skyscrapers of Canary Wharf, before depositing you at Crossharbour or Mudchute stations. Then there's the walk to the farm, skirting the park in which it is set along the main artery of the Isle of Dogs, East Ferry Road, with the still waters of Millwall Outer Dock on the other side of the road – a real marriage of urban, industrial and rural. But mostly it's for the farm's impressive 13 hectares (32 acres). Wandering among the animals and pet corner, encountering everything from large black pigs to piebald Jacob sheep and marvelling at the bright plumage of golden pheasants and mandarin ducks, is just heavenly. Lots of activities ensure little ones won't be bored for even a second, and the insistent presence of the city just adds to the appeal.

—

Pier Street, E14 3HP

www.mudchute.org

Crossharbour or Mudchute DLR

❧ WOOLWICH FERRY

SOUTH-EAST LONDON

Linking Woolwich with North Woolwich and Silvertown in South-East London, this passenger and car ferry service across the River Thames is the best free ride in London. Ferries run frequently daily – just turn up and go – but stop mid-evening (check the Transport for London website for details). In 2019, two new ferries, the *Dame Vera Lynn* (named after the late singer, who was born in East Ham) and the *Ben Woollacott* (to remember a young ferry worker who died on the route) replaced the previous handsome 1960s vessels.

New Ferry Approach, SE18 6DX
or Pier Road, E16 2JS
tfl.gov.uk/modes/river/woolwich-ferry
Woolwich Dockyard rail or King George V DLR

❖ TOWER BRIDGE OPENING

SOUTH-EAST LONDON

One of London's most iconic bridges, Tower Bridge spans the River Thames between the Tower of London on the north bank and Potters Fields Park on the south bank. The bridge never looks more amazing than when it lifts up to allow tall vessels to pass up- or downriver. Check the website for what it calls 'Bridge Lift' times – the 800 or so occasions each year on which local traffic is stopped and Tower Bridge works its magic. On some days the bridge doesn't open at all, while on other days it opens several times, often for the replica paddle steamer *Dixie Queen*, quite a sight in its own right.

Tower Bridge Road, SE1 2UP

www.towerbridge.org.uk/lift-times

Tower Hill tube or Tower Gateway DLR

Coram's Fields

✤ PLAYGROUNDS

CENTRAL LONDON

Coram's Fields (*93 Guilford Street, WC1N 1DN, www.coramsfields.org, Russell Square tube*), in Bloomsbury, is one of the most child-centred places in London – adults are only allowed into the park if they're accompanied by a child. Once inside, there are 2.8 hectares (7 acres) of park and playground to explore, with something for every age group. There are lawns, sandpits, a seasonal paddling pool and a wheelchair-friendly play area. The adventure playground has a zip wire and one of the largest slides in London. There's a little farm too, with goats, rabbits and chickens, plus a wildlife garden. Coram's Fields also runs an organised sports scheme for five- to nineteen-year-olds, ranging from drop-in sessions to tournaments – many of them free.

Across town, in Kensington Gardens, is the Diana Memorial Playground (*Kensington Gardens, W2 4RU, www.royalparks.org.uk, Queensway tube*). It's smaller than Coram's Fields, but children can have a lot of fun here – playing on and around the large wooden pirate ship, and enjoying the sand, teepees and other outdoor play structures. Adults must be accompanied by a child under twelve years old to gain entry.

Diana Memorial Playground

Our Parks

SPORTS ACTIVITIES

London offers a wide number of free health and well-being activities across its parks, gardens and open spaces, from ping-pong tables, petanque courts and bowls to pre-bookable tennis courts, cricket nets, running tracks and football pitches. For our pick of free sociable sports activities, read on.

❖ GYMS
VARIOUS LOCATIONS

Gym-based classes can be expensive, but if you're willing to exercise outdoors, Our Parks (*ourparks.org.uk*) runs group events at a wide range of locations, with all classes led by qualified instructors. Or, for something a bit more challenging, Happy Bootcamps (*www.meetup. com/LondonhappyBootcamps*) in Kensington and Victoria Park offers weekend sessions featuring bodyweight training, running and games.

✤ SKATING

VARIOUS LOCATIONS

Skating through London's streets is huge fun,
which might explain why the marshalled London
Friday Night Skate (*www.lfns.co.uk*) is so popular.
It's fast and furious, but anyone can join in, as long
as you can stop, turn and control your speed on
hills. There's a more relaxed Sunday Stroll, too.

✤ RUNNING

VARIOUS LOCATIONS

Sociable runners will love Parkrun (*www.parkrun. com*) offering 5-kilometre (3-mile) events every Saturday morning at parks across London. London City Runners (*londoncityrunners.com/sessions- and-socials*) goes three better with four runs a week. And if you want to run and do some good, GoodGym (*www.goodgym.org*) mixes running with community projects.

Prudential RideLondon FreeCycle

✤ YOGA
VARIOUS LOCATIONS

Free yoga, pilates and more are a staple of Lululemon (*shop.lululemon.com*) and Sweaty Betty (*www.sweatybetty.com*) shops across the capital, with most of them rolling out the yoga mats for complimentary weekly classes that cater for beginners through to advanced. Both brands also offer other free fitness events, including run clubs, spinning classes, meditation nights, dance, barre and high-intensity interval training (HIIT).

✤ CYCLING
VARIOUS LOCATIONS

Cycling the city's streets can be a daunting prospect for lone leisure cyclists, but the London Cycling Campaign (*lcc.org.uk*) offers a range of group rides, as well as maintenance workshops. And each summer, the Prudential RideLondon FreeCycle (*www.prudentialridelondon.co.uk/ events/freecycle*) gives cyclists the chance to experience the fun and freedom of cycling on traffic-free roads in central London.

❖ MALTBY STREET AND SPA TERMINUS

Borough Market is great, but it's crowded, particularly on Saturdays, so for a more chilled foodie saunter, head east to Maltby Street and Spa Terminus. The railway arches on Maltby Street and Druid Street house some of London's best food and drink suppliers and their presence has encouraged a weekend food market on Ropewalk; more producers can be found a little further south-east in the arches at Spa Terminus (Saturdays only). This is where to keep up with the latest coffee and drink trends, see what's in season and, if you do part with some money, you'll be supporting independent businesses. Further diversion (and temptation) can be found at architectural salvage specialist LASSCO (*37 Maltby Street*).

———

Maltby Street, Ropewalk, Druid Street, Spa Terminus, SE1
www.maltby.st; spa-terminus.co.uk
London Bridge tube/rail

❖ KENSINGTON GARDENS STATUE TRAIL

CENTRAL LONDON

Sometimes a walk is more fun when there are things to tick off along the way, and Kensington Gardens is a handsome park chock-full of statues. Enter the park via Palace Avenue, and start with the statue of King William III, which stands guard outside the south gate of Kensington Palace, before heading around the corner to the marble statue of Queen Victoria, which overlooks the Round Pond. Walk eastwards to see GF Watts's imposing *Physical Energy*, a bronze of a man on horseback, and remember to look over the Long Water for a great view of Henry Moore's *The Arch* in Hyde Park. Then head north to see *Peter Pan*, a bronze statue commissioned by JM Barrie himself, and a favourite with children, who will also like the Two Bears Fountain near the Italian Gardens. Here you'll also find the statue of Edward Jenner, inventor of the smallpox vaccine. Loop back south via the Speke Monument, a red granite obelisk erected to explorer John Hanning Speke, and finish with a flourish at the Albert Memorial – a gleaming, golden tribute from Queen Victoria to her husband Albert.

Palace Avenue, W8 4PT
www.royalparks.org.uk/parks/kensington-gardens
High Street Kensington tube

✣ THE GARDEN AT 120

THE CITY

Opened in February 2019, the rooftop garden at 120 Fenchurch Street is something special. The design, by landscape architects Latz+Partner, is captivating. A considered mix of flowers, grasses and wisteria-clad pergolas, plus contemporary water features and seating areas, make it a genuinely relaxing spot. Take sandwiches and spend some time gazing down on the City. Wander around the garden to see amazing views in all directions, as well as close-ups of the Gherkin, the Walkie Talkie and the Lloyds Building. Back at ground level, there's a bonus art treat in *The Call of Things*, a mesmerising art installation by Vong Phaophanit and Claire Oboussier. Go mid-morning or in the afternoon to avoid queuing; bags are put through a scanner, then a fast lift takes you to the fifteenth floor. You don't have to book, but do check the website before you go – the rooftop is sometimes closed for private events.

----

120 Fenchurch Street, EC3M 5BA
www.thegardenat120.com
Fenchurch Street rail

✣ PORTOBELLO MARKET
WEST LONDON

Friday is the best day to visit this classic London market, when there are masses of vintage fashion stalls in the section under the Westway. Start at the southern end of Portobello Road and marvel at the chi-chi houses; walk swiftly past the tourist-trap antiques stalls that line the beginning of the market, towards the more rackety charms near the Westway and Golborne Road. Here the stalls sport a fascinating mix of old tat and covetable knick-knacks, with everything from brown furniture and battered leather coats to heaps of jewellery and piles of plates. There's always something to catch the eye. There are also some interesting shops to browse in: the Spice Shop (*1 Blenheim Crescent*), Books for Cooks (*4 Blenheim Crescent*) and The Cloth Shop (*290 Portobello Road*) are particularly tempting. Walk further, and on to Golborne Road, where old-time bric-a-brac stalls are pitched outside high-end antiques shops. Here, also, is the final temptation – Portuguese coffee shops Café O'Porto (No. 62) and Lisboa Patisserie (No. 57).

—

Portobello Road, W10, W11; Golborne Road, W10
www.portobelloroad.co.uk
Notting Hill or Ladbroke Grove tube

FOUNTAINS

London's fountains can be a godsend in the summer heat of the city. Just sitting near their cooling waters can reinvigorate during a lunch hour. Some offer kids (and grown-ups) hours of fun running among the jets or paddling in the pools. Here are six of our favourites.

❖ SOUTH BANK

CENTRAL LONDON

Jeppe Hein's *Appearing Rooms* has been thrilling summer visitors to the South Bank since 2006. Exhibiting his trademark playfulness, jets create walls of water that appear and disappear to make the rooms of its title – the trick being to stand among the jets anticipating which will suddenly shoot into life and nimbly avoiding them.

—

Belvedere Road, SE1 8XX
www.southbankcentre.co.uk
Waterloo tube/rail

26

✢ GRANARY SQUARE
CENTRAL LONDON

Similar in design to Hein's *Appearing Rooms*, but on a larger scale, Granary Square's modern fountain features 1,080 individually controlled and choreographed water jets that appear and disappear randomly, changing height as they do so. Nearby seating means parents can happily watch over kids as they play. Come dusk the jets are lit up in bright colours.

—

Granary Square, N1C 4PQ
King's Cross St Pancras tube/rail

✢ SOMERSET HOUSE
CENTRAL LONDON

Being surrounded by the elegant nineteenth-century architecture of Somerset House is reason enough to visit the Edmond J Safra Fountain Court, but the presence of its fifty-five water jets is an added bonus. It's popular year-round, but not always open, closing for annual events such as Film4 Summer Screen and winter ice-skating.

—

The Strand, WC2R 1LA
www.somersethouse.org.uk
Temple tube

Diana Memorial Fountain

✤ VICTORIA AND ALBERT MUSEUM
WEST LONDON

The V&A's Italianate inner courtyard is a gorgeous place in which to take an art break. Dotted around its calming oval pool, fringed with water jets and reached by a few shallow steps, is a café, making this a great spot for watchful grown-ups and their little ones. Lemon trees complete the very pretty picture.

—

Cromwell Road, SW7 2RL
www.vam.ac.uk
South Kensington tube

✤ DIANA MEMORIAL FOUNTAIN
CENTRAL LONDON

A perfect splashing-about-in fountain, thanks to its stream-like design, three bridges, a calm pool and a livelier gurgling brook element (apparently representing the two sides to the princess's life). Visitors are asked to refrain from entering the waters, though it's fine to sit on the edges and cool your feet in them.

—

West Carriage Drive, W2 2UH
www.royalparks.org.uk
Lancaster Gate tube

✤ BARBICAN CENTRE
THE CITY

Concrete pads bordering the expansive brutalist lake at the Barbican Centre make it a fantastic spot for a lunchtime cool-off in the city heat. The terrace café facing onto it has lots of good lunch options, but watch out for the resident ducks who might want a share of whatever it is you're having.

—

Silk Street, EC2Y 8DS
www.barbican.org.uk
Barbican tube

Victoria and Albert Museum

Barbican Centre

❖ GOLDERS HILL PARK ZOO

<u>NORTH LONDON</u>

Open to the public since 1898 and connected to Hampstead Heath, North London's Golders Hill Park would simply be a pleasant neighbourhood park, were it not for one unique feature – a free zoo. Granted, the zoo is not huge, but it is clearly very well managed, and the animals – small mammals such as donkeys, ring-tailed coati and lemurs – alongside a diverse range of birds that include European eagle owls, laughing kookaburras and white-faced whistling ducks (most of which are available for adoption), all look very comfortable. There's a butterfly house too, as well as rheas and fallow deer with plenty of roaming space, while a stumpery is home to a lot of cheeky near-tame squirrels who'll eat monkey nuts from your hand if you want to get really close to the not-so-wild life. Tennis courts, a pond crossed via a humped bridge, a play area, a café, a fern-filled sunken garden, woodland and a pergola complete a very pretty picture.

—

North End Way, NW3 7HE

www.cityoflondon.gov.uk/things-to-do/green-spaces/hampstead-heath/golders-hill-park

Golders Green tube

❖ COLUMBIA ROAD FLOWER MARKET

EAST LONDON

One of London's most Instagrammable events, this street market was established decades before social media made it one of the city's biggest draws, and it still has the wow factor. It's partly due to the plants and flowers, which sing out with colour year-round, but it's also special for the repartee and banter of the East London sellers, many of whom have had stalls here for decades and whose exhortations to buy 'faaaaave bunches uh tulips for uh fiver' create a lively atmosphere. That atmosphere has been a feature of this road since the nineteenth century, when social reformer and philanthropist Angela Burdett-Coutts established a covered food market (with a whopping 400 stalls) along it, which eventually became the Sunday-only flower market, open from 8am–2pm. Since then, bijou shops offering bagels, coffee, vintage homeware, art and lots more have added appeal to hungry visitors and browsers.

Columbia Road, E2 7RG

www.columbiaroad.info

Hoxton overground

33

Thames Path at Richmond

BEST THAMESIDE WALKS

Twickenham to Richmond (north bank)
Highlights: Eel Pie Island, York House Italian Fountain, Orleans House, Marble Hill Park

Chiswick to Fulham (north bank)
Highlights: Chiswick Mall and Upper Mall, Chiswick Eyot, Hammersmith Bridge, Fulham Palace and Gardens

Wandsworth to Battersea (south bank)
Highlights: Battersea Heliport, St Mary's church, Peace Pagoda, Battersea Park

Lambeth to Waterloo (south bank)
Highlights: views of the Houses of Parliament and central London sights, street entertainers, National Theatre River Stage (summer)

Tower of London to Limehouse (north bank)
Highlights: Tower Bridge, St Katherine's Dock, Wapping Old Stairs, Limehouse Basin

Cutty Sark to Woolwich Ferry (south bank)
Highlights: Greenwich Foot Tunnel, Greenwich Peninsula Ecology Park, Thames Barrier, Woolwich Ferry

2

GREEN
SPACES

✤ THAMES BARRIER PARK

EAST LONDON

What a special, understated park this is; a small space stretching between the DLR station of Pontoon Dock and the Thames, with some greenery and a little playground, but seemingly not much else. Step inside it though, and all sorts of intriguing features begin to show themselves. Here is the elegant Pavilion of Peace, designed by Andrew Taylor as a memorial to Redbridge residents who died in wars. Just beyond it, a viewing point offers some excellent and unusual downriver views of the Thames Barrier. And nearby, a modest park café provides a restful spot for a cuppa. But it's the Green Dock, a sunken garden undulating with waves of yew hedging and pretty planting, that is the park's USP, a lovely feature criss-crossed by two bridges enabling a great view on to the plants and wildlife below. Lovingly tended, it's a particularly arresting sight when ablaze with colour in spring.

North Woolwich Road, E16 2HP

www.london.gov.uk/what-we-do/environment/parks-green-spaces-and-biodiversity/parks-and-green-spaces/thames-barrier-park

Pontoon Dock DLR

✤ POSTMAN'S PARK

THE CITY

The park is a welcome green spot in the City, but the reason to make a special trip is the Watts Memorial to Heroic Self-Sacrifice. Established in 1900, this wall of glazed Doulton tiles is a tribute to people who perished while saving others, such as Alice Ayres, who saved three children from a burning building in Borough in 1885. It makes grim reading: the earliest case (1885) is that of pantomime artiste Sarah Smith who died of

'terrible injuries received when attempting in her inflammable dress to extinguish the flames which had enveloped her companion'. Most accounts are Victorian, but a new plaque was added in 2009, dedicated to Leigh Pitt who died while saving a child from drowning. The name of the park? The old General Post Office used to be next door.

—

King Edward Street, EC1A 7BT
www.cityoflondon.gov.uk/things-to-do/city-gardens/
find-a-garden/postmans-park
St Paul's tube

✤ FULHAM PALACE HOUSE AND GARDEN

SOUTH-WEST LONDON

For many centuries Fulham Palace was the country retreat of the bishops of London, but now it offers all-comers entertainment and relaxation in the form of a Thames-side mansion and a 5-hectare (13-acre) garden. The grounds contain some rare and majestic trees (including a 500-year-old holm oak, one of the oldest in Britain), a peaceful walled garden and generous lawns for running around or picnicking. There's also a natural play area for children and various family fun days, plus exhibitions, tours and talks for adults, all of which are free. The Tudor courtyard is a must-see, but the whole house is worth exploring — it's been beautifully restored in the last few years.

—

Bishop's Avenue, SW6 6EA

www.fulhampalace.org

Putney Bridge tube

✤ GREENWICH PENINSULA ECOLOGY PARK

SOUTH-EAST LONDON

Readers of *A Serpent's Tail* might well feel they've stepped into its pages in this ethereal space. Hard by a wide-curving stretch of the Thames just downriver of the Thames Barrier, the park's sense of otherness is palpable; it feels ancient and Fen-like rather than modern and distinctly London-like. And packed in its 1.6 hectares (4 acres) of marshland, two lakes and Alder woodland fringe are plenty of natural wonders you'd be hard-pressed to find anywhere else in the area, including a wildflower meadow. Child-friendly wildlife includes newts, frogs, butterflies and, of course, birds – reed warblers, swifts, snipes and water rail among them – which can be viewed close-up from two bird hides. Near the entrance, the upscale and health-focused Café Pura serves a great range of veggie-centric food as well as snacks and drinks.

—

John Harrison Way, SE10 0QZ
www.tcv.org.uk/greenwichpeninsula
North Greenwich tube

✤ CRYSTAL PALACE PARK

It's hard not to love a park that boasts a set of dinosaur sculptures. Dating from 1854, the beasts are arranged around a large pond at the southern end of the park; they're factually inaccurate, but strangely appealing. More kid-friendly reasons to visit Crystal Palace Park include a skatepark, a maze and the hilly terrain, which is made for running up and rolling down. The handsome ruins of Crystal Palace itself dominate the park, and there are amazing views from its terraces. Children will also appreciate the collection of red sphinxes to be found up there. The park is a lovely place just to walk, too, with plenty of ancient trees and a variety of lakes and ponds, the most peaceful of which lies in front of the strikingly modern, if rather neglected, open-air concert platform. If you come on a Sunday, the park museum is open, and you can find out more about the giant glasshouse that gave the area its name – designed by Sir Joseph Paxton for the 1851 Great Exhibition in Hyde Park, then moved to South-East London, it finally burned down in a spectacular fire in 1936. Extend your stroll beyond the perimeter by following the clearly signposted Green Chain or Capital Ring routes out of the park.

—

Thicket Road, SE20 8DT
crystalpalacepark.org.uk
Crystal Palace rail

✤ WOODBERRY WETLANDS

NORTH LONDON

Created out of the old Stoke Newington reservoirs, Woodberry Wetlands is a little piece of bucolic bliss in an otherwise densely populated area of North London. Covering 11 hectares (27 acres), it's a haven for wildlife, with birds, bats, butterflies, frogs and more making the area their home, not to mention foxes. The variety of birdlife is huge, as wetlands attract many migrating species alongside the year-round residents. Depending on the time of year, you might spot anything from swallows and warblers to terns and buzzards, and there are often sightings of rarer birds – you can check the notice boards for news of the latest spottings. Kingfishers breed here, so you might even see a flash of iridescent colour. In summer, you'll definitely spot dragonflies hovering over the water. All this wildlife means no dogs are allowed. The top floor of the Coal House Café offers a great vantage point for taking it all in.

———

Bethune Road, N16 5HQ
www.woodberrywetlands.org.uk
Manor House tube

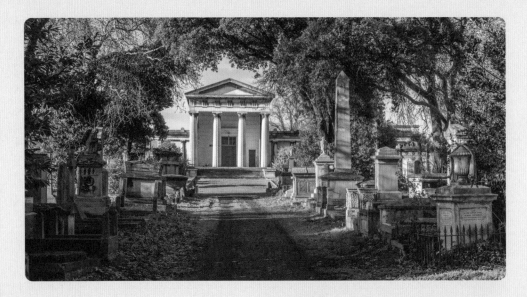

LONDON CEMETERIES

London's rapid population growth in the nineteenth century led to calls for more burial grounds, and a series of mega-cemeteries — the so-called Magnificent Seven — followed in quick succession. Highgate Cemetery, the big-hitter in terms of names and monuments, charges an entrance fee, but the other six are free to enter: all are atmospheric spaces with amazing memorials.

✤ KENSAL GREEN CEMETERY
WEST LONDON

The first of the Magnificent Seven to be built, in 1833, this 29-hectare (72-acre) site beside the Grand Union Canal is a wildlife haven as well as a working cemetery. Authors Wilkie Collins and Anthony Trollope, and engineer Isambard Kingdom Brunel, are buried here, as is the French acrobat and tightrope walker Charles Blondin.

—

Harrow Road, W10 4RA
www.kensalgreen.co.uk
Kensal Green tube

✤ WEST NORWOOD CEMETERY
SOUTH-EAST LONDON

Consecrated in 1837, the 16-hectare (40-acre) cemetery was designed by Sir William Tite in the Gothic Revival style and has almost seventy listed monuments. Many are in need of some TLC, and a five-year restoration project started in 2019. Don't miss the terracotta and pottery tile mausoleum of Sir Henry Doulton (of Royal Doulton fame).

—

Norwood Road, SE27 9JU
www.fownc.org
West Norwood rail

✤ ABNEY PARK CEMETERY
NORTH LONDON

Abney Park had strong links with dissenters and the semi-derelict Gothic building at its centre is Europe's oldest surviving non-denominational chapel. The most appealing monument here is that to Frank Bostock. A well-known showman and wild animal trainer, he died in 1912 and is buried beneath a magnificent marble lion.

—

215 Stoke Newington High Street, N16 0LH
abneypark.org
Stoke Newington rail

✤ TOWER HAMLETS CEMETERY

EAST LONDON

Established in 1841, Tower Hamlets Cemetery is now run as a park, and has a greater variety of habitats than the other cemeteries – wildflowers, ponds, aged trees and open spaces as well as bosky, overgrown areas. An active Friends group runs the park and is behind all kinds of initiatives, including a Heritage Trail that takes in notable memorials.

——

Southern Grove, E3 4PX

www.fothcp.org

Mile End tube

✤ BROMPTON CEMETERY

SOUTH-WEST LONDON

The only one of the Magnificent Seven to be run by the Royal Parks, Brompton is also the most manicured. Suffragette Emmeline Pankhurst is buried here; her arts and crafts memorial can be found near the Old Brompton Road entrance. Some say Beatrix Potter found inspiration for names here: look out for Nutkin, Fisher and McGregor among the 35,000 graves and monuments.

——

Fulham Road, SW10 9UG

www.royalparks.org.uk/parks/brompton-cemetery

Fulham Broadway tube

✤ NUNHEAD CEMETERY
SOUTH-EAST LONDON

The 21 hectares (52 acres) of Nunhead Cemetery are an attractive mix of open, formal walkways and overgrown paths, plus some heavily wooded areas. A number of music hall stars are buried here, as are the young victims of the 'Leysdown Tragedy' – Scouts whose boat overturned on a sailing trip to the Isle of Sheppey. Don't leave without appreciating the view of St Paul's Cathedral.

—

Linden Grove, SE15 3LP
www.fonc.org.uk
Nunhead rail

✤ QUEEN ELIZABETH OLYMPIC PARK

EAST LONDON

In the medal table of Olympic Park legacies, London's 2012 games site surely takes gold. Developed from a huge area spanning the boroughs of Hackney, Newham, Tower Hamlets and Waltham Forest, what was once a blight on the landscape of East London is now settling down very nicely into that landscape. Colourful high-rise blocks, a football stadium, an aquatics centre designed by Zaha Hadid and a giant red slide by Anish Kapoor are just some of the unusual elements to be found here. But none of them convey why it's such a special place in which to spend an hour, a day or anything in between. Perhaps it's simply the strong sense of being in the city while walking through landscaped gardens, wildflower meadows and tree walks, or meandering along the banks of the River Lea, or playing in the Tumbling Bay playground, or riding pell-mell up and down the mountain bike trails, or shrieking with laughter as you run among the 195 coloured fountain jets of the Water Labyrinth.

Stratford, E20

www.queenelizabetholympicpark.co.uk

Stratford tube/overground/rail

Queen Elizabeth's Hunting Lodge

✤ EPPING FOREST

EAST LONDON

Where best to begin with Epping Forest? Deciding how to tackle this former royal forest can be a daunting prospect. A good starting point is Chingford rail station, from where a number of walks take in the famed Queen Elizabeth's Hunting Lodge (*8 Rangers Road, E4 7QH*) as well as offering easy access to one of the forest's super-useful visitor centres. From here, numerous walks of all lengths and difficulty levels take in many of Epping's top sites, including Connaught Water, Strawberry Hill Ponds, peaceful swathes of ancient woodland, scrubby flatlands and the excellent

Original Tea Hut (*Fairmead Road, IG10 4HR*), known to everyone as the biker's café. The walk you choose depends on who's with you. Grown-ups might want to skirt the family-attracting lakes where the local wildlife tucks into forest-approved duck food (available from the two visitor centres). Alternatively, you could strike out along any number of smaller trails criss-crossing the forest to spots such as Copped Hall (*Crown Hill, CM16 5HS*), where the deer are understandably popular with both adults and children.

———

Chingford, E4

www.visiteppingforest.org

Chingford rail

✤ HOLLAND PARK

WEST LONDON

A trip to Holland Park is a trip to a fantasy London, where wedding-cake white mansions and winsome children with beatific nannies evoke the world of Mary Poppins. Young oligarchs jog along the paths, wholesome-looking youths play tennis or get together for cricket practice, and grandparents work on their putting . . . sound annoying? It's utterly delightful. Part of the park's appeal is its variety. A Japanese-style Kyoto Garden is centred around a pond with a waterfall. Large expanses of lawn are great for picnics. A moss-covered, tiered garden resembles something out of an Indiana Jones movie. And around them all wind woodland paths bordered by planting that brings colour even in the depths of winter. But it's in summer that the park excels, with children's play areas and the café packed to the rafters. The likes of Lord Byron, Benjamin Disraeli, Charles Dickens and Sir Walter Scott have enjoyed this beautiful space since the nineteenth century; follow in their footsteps and you'll have a glorious time.

Ilchester Place, W8 6LU

www.rbkc.gov.uk/leisure-and-culture/parks/holland-park

Holland Park tube

BIG GREEN SPACES

Regent's Park, NW1

Swathes of grass, charming formal gardens and four children's playgrounds – amid sounds from London Zoo
www.royalparks.org.uk/parks/the-regents-park
Regent's Park tube

Hampstead Heath, NW3

Woods, water and wildness, spread over a glorious 320 hectares (790 acres)
www.cityoflondon.gov.uk/things-to-do/green-spaces/hampstead-heath
Hampstead Heath tube/overground or Gospel Oak overground

Victoria Park, E3

The 'lungs of East London', complete with a canal-side walk and a skate park
www.towerhamlets.gov.uk/lgnl/leisure_and_culture/parks_and_open_spaces/victoria_park
Hackney Wick overground

Battersea Park, SW11

Thameside park with a boating lake, a pagoda and an art gallery
www.wandsworth.gov.uk/batterseapark
Battersea Park overground/rail

Greenwich Park, SE10

Elegant, historic park; home to the meridian line and a small herd of deer
www.royalparks.org.uk/parks/greenwich-park
Cutty Sark DLR or Maze Hill rail

Hyde Park, W2

With London's oldest boating lake, the Serpentine, and a lovely rose garden
www.royalparks.org.uk/parks/hyde-park
Hyde Park Corner/ Marble Arch tube

Richmond Park, TW10

Heathland, ancient trees and herds of deer, plus the stunning Isabella Plantation garden
www.royalparks.org.uk/parks/richmond-park
Richmond tube/overground/rail

3

MUSEUMS

✤ SIR JOHN SOANE'S MUSEUM

<u>CENTRAL LONDON</u>

Lincoln's Inn Fields is a Georgian gem.
And, surprisingly, it's often quieter than it
might have been in Georgian days, the ornate
gates of its townhouses rarely troubled by
visitors. This makes it easy to spot the Sir John
Soane's Museum, usually identifiable by its small
queue of visitors or frequent comings and goings.
To wander the higgledy-piggledy rooms of the
Regency architect's former home, filled with
artefacts amassed travelling the globe, is to be
confronted at every turn by classical period finds
piled on top of each other in their thousands.
They range from Egyptian antiquities and Roman
sculpture to elephants' teeth and mummified
cats. The absence of labels and cabinets makes it
feel very much like a curious old hoarder's house,
if said old hoarder had a passion for architectural
ephemera. Before his death Soane took steps
to ensure the space be preserved for future
generations to enjoy and be educated by, for
free, and forever. Long may his legacy survive.

----

13 Lincoln's Inn Fields, WC2A 3BP
www.soane.org
Holborn tube

❖ WELLCOME COLLECTION

CENTRAL LONDON

The Wellcome Collection opened in 2007, its stated aim to challenge how we think and feel about health. More than thirteen years on, via a collection exhibited over two absorbing permanent exhibitions, plus an eclectic series of temporary shows and events, it's still managing to do just that, in a modern, light-filled and forward-thinking space. Shows here are happy to probe every area of the body and mind, from the psychology of magic to the treatment of mental health via personal responses to cancer and votive art.

Never less than reflective and thoughtful, they deal with health and well-being in intelligent yet accessible ways that manage to tread a fine line between information, entertainment and engagement without simplification or an over-reliance on gadgets and interaction. That's not to say there is not a lot of playfulness here; there often is, and generally pitched at just the right level for a tricky audience, which for any given exhibition will span generations.

----

183 Euston Road, NW1 2BE
wellcomecollection.org
Euston tube/rail

❖ KENWOOD HOUSE

NORTH LONDON

Kenwood House is a double whammy, as the recently restored mini-stately home holds a renowned art collection. The location, at the edge of Hampstead Heath, doesn't hurt either. The house was remodelled by Robert Adam into a neoclassical masterpiece in the eighteenth century; the ceilings in particular are glorious, especially the one by Antonio Zucchi in the library. The paintings, donated by brewing magnate Edward Guinness (known as the Iveagh Bequest), include Rembrandt's *Self-Portrait with Two Circles* and works by Gainsborough, Vermeer and Reynolds. There are dressing-up and play areas for children, who will also be entertained by oddities such as an early wheelchair and a set of ingenious library steps. The garden is also worth a look – it was designed by Humphry Repton – and contains some attractive old dairy buildings, which are open to the public on occasional weekends.

—

Hampstead Lane, NW3 7JR

www.english-heritage.org.uk/visit/places/kenwood

Archway tube then 210 bus

❖ LONDON MITHRAEUM BLOOMBERG SPACE

THE CITY

Set in a small corner of Sir Norman Foster's 2018 Stirling Prize-winning Bloomberg European HQ, the London Mithraeum offers two contrasting takes on creativity spanning almost two millennia. On the ground floor, changing exhibitions present work that responds to the star of the show beneath it, the Roman remains of the London Mithraeum, or Temple of Mithras. Entry numbers are restricted so you may have a short wait to see the cleverly presented remains of the third-century temple's structure, with reconstructions of key sculptures that were found when it was excavated at a nearby site in 1954 (the originals are in the Museum of London, page 81). While you're waiting, staff will proffer interactive guides to a floor-to-ceiling glass cabinet filled with jewellery, pottery, glass works, coins and weapons, just a small but fascinatingly representative selection of the more than 14,000 artefacts found at the excavation site. It brings the temple to life for young and old, and rounds off the experience perfectly.

—

12 Walbrook, EC4N 8AA

www.londonmithraeum.com

Bank tube

❧ HOGARTH'S HOUSE

WEST LONDON

William Hogarth bought this small house in 1749 as a country retreat, but it's hard to imagine today, with cars roaring past on the A4 just the other side of the garden wall. Once inside, the atmosphere is altogether more convivial; personal artefacts and examples of his work, helpfully annotated, give a sense of the acclaimed painter, engraver and satirist, and his circle. Prints on display include the sets depicting *A Rake's Progress* and *Marriage à la Mode*, as well as *Gin Lane*, none of which pull any punches about the society Hogarth saw around him. His tomb is in the graveyard of St Nicholas church, about five minutes' walk from the house; head there to get some idea of the charming village atmosphere that once prevailed in Chiswick.

Hogarth Lane, Great West Road, W4 2QN

www.hounslow.gov.uk

Turnham Green tube

❖ HORNIMAN MUSEUM AND GARDENS

SOUTH-EAST LONDON

A delightful one-off, the Horniman has something for everyone, with collections ranging across natural history, anthropology and musical instruments. There are stuffed animals, fossils, shells, paintings, ceramics, clothing, masks and headdresses, and ancient artefacts that make you ask 'what is that?'. The striking arts and crafts building is backed by lovely gardens, and fronted by London's first Alaskan totem pole. Check the website for details of the many free drop-in workshops and talks, but note that there's a charge for the Butterfly House, the Aquarium and some of the temporary exhibitions. The Horniman is one of the most child-friendly museums in London, so be aware that weekends and school holidays can be hectic.

---

100 London Road, SE23 3PQ
www.horniman.ac.uk
Forest Hill rail

✤ RAF MUSEUM

NORTH LONDON

Spread over several hangars on the site of the old Hendon aerodrome, the RAF Museum is both spacious and information packed, with lots of interactive exhibits – test your reaction times, or your plotting skills. And then there are the planes: beautiful objects in their own right, as well as marvels of engineering, many of them have fascinating histories; the gleaming 1930s Supermarine Stranraer, for example, was one of the world's last biplane flying boats. There's a selection of support vehicles – including classic motorcycles, transporters and in-flight refuellers – plus ephemera, such as a 1925 teddy bear complete with knitted uniform. A great venue for kids, the RAF Museum has a picnic area, cafés, open spaces and an outdoor play area.

Grahame Park Way, NW9 5LL

www.rafmuseum.org.uk/london

Colindale tube

✤ GRANT MUSEUM OF ZOOLOGY
CENTRAL LONDON

The Grant Museum is one of those places that, once visited, is never forgotten. And with good reason. Founded in 1827, this University College London museum houses more than 68,000 zoological specimens spanning the entire animal kingdom, in a space packed to the rafters with display cases filled with skeletons, models and stuffed creatures, jars of specimens in spirit, and shelves bursting with the most esoteric and wondrous exhibits imaginable. Here is a glass jar crammed with moles (unsurprisingly a firm favourite with visitors, many of whom try to fathom just how many moles are in there), there some dodo bones, and everywhere something you're almost sure never to have seen before. The museum runs a lively programme of events that includes a range of family activities, guided tours and openings on the last Thursday of the month, when UCL Lates bring interactive and live events to the space.

—

Rockefeller Building, 21 University Street, WC1E 6DE
www.ucl.ac.uk/culture/grant-museum-zoology
Euston Square or Warren Street tube

✣ PETRIE MUSEUM OF EGYPTIAN ARCHAEOLOGY

<u>CENTRAL LONDON</u>

Like its natural-world counterpart the Grant Museum of Zoology, this University College London museum offers a cornucopia of wonders – an estimated 80,000 of them – but this time focused on Egyptian and Sudanese archaeology. And also like the Grant, its close-packed objects and artefacts detailing life in the Nile Valley from prehistory to the Islamic period offer delightful finds at every turn. Drawn from a wide number of archaeological sites are an impressive number of 'firsts', among them one of the earliest pieces of linen from Egypt, a dancer's dress from around 2400 BCE, and a lot of sewing needles; in bone, wood, bronze, copper – the Egyptians clearly liked their fashion. The creativity continues with colourful tiles, carvings and frescoes, jewellery, stoneware and glassware. Feast on it all, and thank the memory of the woman who made it happen back in 1892, when it was established via a bequest from the traveller and diarist Amelia Edwards.

—

Malet Place, WC1E 6BT

www.ucl.ac.uk/culture/petrie-museum

Euston Square tube

⚜ BANK OF ENGLAND MUSEUM

THE CITY

If this sounds like a dry and dusty experience, think again. There's much to interest visitors, with plenty of 'I didn't know that . . .' moments. Scores of famous people have had connections to the bank: composer George Frideric Handel held two accounts here; and Kenneth Grahame, author of *The Wind in the Willows*, held a senior position at the bank – there's a charming display devoted to the book, and a startling description of an attempt on his life. The Banknote Gallery includes counterfeit notes from Operation Bernhard, a Nazi plot to destabilise the pound during World War II, and the workings of the modern bank are explained in a short video narrated by Stephen Fry. There are lovely things to look at, too: from real gold bars to artefacts such as the handsome old cash register from the staff canteen, replaced after decimalisation in 1971 (good luck explaining the pre-decimal system to anyone under 50).

—

Bartholomew Lane, EC2R 8AH

www.bankofengland.co.uk/museum

Bank tube

✣ BRITISH LIBRARY

CENTRAL LONDON

A fraction of the British Library's 170 million-strong collection is on show here, but these highlights are something else. There are maps, letters, documents, books and ephemera, covering art, science, music, sacred texts and historical documents. Visitors can see Paul McCartney's handwritten lyrics for 'Yesterday', and then listen to the song at an audio post, or marvel at Charlotte Brontë's miniscule lettering, and hear James Joyce read an excerpt from *Finnegans Wake*. There are music scores by Mozart, early collections of Shakespeare's plays and poems, and notebooks by Leonardo da Vinci. Illustrated books run from Javanese manuscripts and European Books of Hours to contemporary artists' books. Some objects are poignant, such as suffragette Olive Wharry's scrapbook, and some awe-inspiring – the mighty Magna Carta dates from 1215. Just outside the main exhibition, on the upper-ground floor, are the Philatelic Collections, with cases of banknotes and rare stamps.

----

96 Euston Road, NW1 2DB

www.bl.uk

King's Cross St Pancras tube/rail

✤ QUEEN'S HOUSE
SOUTH-EAST LONDON

Reopened in February 2020 after a splendid revamp, the Queen's House is full of treasures. There's a stellar collection of paintings – with an emphasis on maritime art – ranging from the *Armada Portrait of Elizabeth I* to LS Lowry's *View of Deptford Power Station from Greenwich*, plus modern acquisitions such as Kehinde Wiley's *Ship of Fools*. But there are also fascinating artefacts, including model ships, figureheads, arts and crafts De Morgan ware and grandfather clocks. And then there's the house itself, designed by Inigo Jones: the exquisite Tulip staircase and the stunning Great Hall are the stand-out elements, but the views, south over the park and the Royal Observatory, and north to the Thames and the Royal Naval College, are top-notch too. Keep an eye out for free talks and, on Wednesdays, lunchtime concerts.

Romney Road, SE10 9NF
www.rmg.co.uk/queens-house
Cutty Sark DLR or Maze Hill rail

Science Museum

MAGNIFICENT MUSEUMS

British Museum, WC1
The story of humankind, told through a permanent collection of more than eight million artefacts.
www.britishmuseum.org
Holborn tube

Natural History Museum, SW7
Thousands of fascinating exhibits – including dinosaur skeletons – set across soaring halls and beautiful spaces.
www.nhm.ac.uk
South Kensington tube

Science Museum, SW7
Hands-on science across interactive areas and more than 15,000 objects.
www.sciencemuseum.org.uk
South Kensington tube

Victoria and Albert Museum, SW7
A decorative arts collection that's arguably one of the best in the world.
www.vam.ac.uk
South Kensington tube

Imperial War Museum, SE1
Lively and accessible displays tell stories of modern conflict, from WWI to the present day.
www.iwm.org.uk
Elephant & Castle tube/rail or Lambeth North tube

National Maritime Museum, SE10
Britain's naval history engagingly documented at a site that takes in the *Cutty Sark*.
www.rmg.co.uk/national-maritime-museum
Cutty Sark DLR or Maze Hill rail

Museum of London, EC2
Interactive displays detail the city's evolution from prehistoric times to the present day.
www.museumoflondon.org.uk
Barbican tube

Museum of Childhood, E2
Closed until 2022, it will reopen as 'a world-leading centre of creativity for children'.
www.vam.ac.uk/moc
Bethnal Green tube

4

GALLERIES

✤ WHITECHAPEL GALLERY

EAST LONDON

Set on the grungy Whitechapel Road in East London, this venerable century-old space feels quite different to its surroundings, but its ethos is very much around engagement with the local community, with education and in organising programmes that make art here accessible to young and old. The solo shows mounted since the space opened in 1902 read like a greatest hits of modern art – Pablo Picasso's *Guernica* was displayed here in 1932, for its one and only visit to Britain, and other premieres have included Frida Kahlo and Jackson Pollock. A thoughtful roster of themed shows is equally impressive, as are the events. With the exception of two annual ticketed shows that support the exhibition and education programmes, all exhibitions are free, as are many of the events, from family-friendly activities and talks and screenings to curators' tours and Thursday Late performances.

—

77–82 Whitechapel High Street, E1 7QX
www.whitechapelgallery.org
Aldgate East tube

✤ SERPENTINE GALLERIES

CENTRAL LONDON

The beautiful Hyde Park setting is enough of a draw to the two buildings that make up the Serpentine Galleries – the Serpentine Gallery and the Serpentine Sackler Gallery – even without the art. Inside, always challenging, but enjoyable exhibitions have pushed the boundaries of art presentation by championing and pioneering conceptual and multidisciplinary art and artists for more than fifty years. A glance over the archive reveals names that are far from household ones – Cerith Wyn Evans, Pierre Huyghe,

Rose Wylie – but are much admired in the art world. And it's not just in art that these galleries push the boundaries; architecture is integral to the programme here, with the opening of the annual Serpentine Pavilion an eagerly awaited event each summer. More than two decades on from Zaha Hadid's inaugural pavilion of 2000, these eloquent, elegant temporary structures by architects from all over the globe have never failed to amaze.

Kensington Gardens, W2 3XA

www.serpentinegalleries.org

Lancaster Gate tube

✜ THE PHOTOGRAPHERS' GALLERY

CENTRAL LONDON

This is a gem of a gallery, with first-rate shows and free admission for members and under-18s. The Photographers' Gallery was the first to show such names as Andreas Gursky and Sebastião Salgado in Britain. Celebrating its 50th anniversary in 2021, the gallery maintains its position as the UK's leading photography gallery with a mix of new and retrospective work; 'Shot in Soho' celebrated the area's diverse and dynamic culture and showcased well-known names (Corinne Day, William Klein) alongside less famous ones. The annual Deutsche Börse Photography Foundation Prize, which features four current artists exploring photography-based practices is always worth seeing. The gallery offers creative career talks and workshops with its Develop programme for 14–24 year olds, and a dynamic Media Wall, unpacking digital considerations in photography with its Digital Programme.

—

16–18 Ramillies Street, W1F 7LW

thephotographersgallery.org.uk

Oxford Circus tube

Clancy Gebler Davies, *The Colony Rooms*, 1999–2000

⚜ GUILDHALL ART GALLERY AND LONDON'S ROMAN AMPHITHEATRE
THE CITY

Despite holding a number of impressive works, the Guildhall Art Gallery feels like undiscovered treasure – maybe because it's tucked away in Guildhall Yard – and the lack of crowds makes it a rare treat for visitors. The gallery shows a selection of the City of London Corporation's vast collection, including one of the largest oil paintings in Britain, John Singleton Copley's *Defeat of the Floating Batteries at Gibraltar*, and a number of glorious Pre-Raphaelite works, notably Dante Gabriel Rossetti's *La Ghirlandata*. Many of the paintings are of London scenes and themes. The building also holds the remains of a Roman amphitheatre, cleverly brought to life with digital projections.

Guildhall Yard, EC2V 5AE

www.guildhall.cityoflondon.gov.uk/art-gallery

Bank tube

❖ WILLIAM MORRIS GALLERY

EAST LONDON

This likeable local gallery is based in what was designer William Morris's home as a young man (1848–1856). There's plenty of work on display – books, ceramics, stained glass, designs for fabrics and wallpapers – by Morris and his arts and crafts associates (particularly Edward Burne-Jones and Dante Gabriel Rossetti), and the special exhibitions are always worth seeing.

Space is also given to a collection of artist-craftsman Frank Brangwyn's work, ranging across paintings, drawings, stained-glass designs and murals. The gallery doubles as a community hub, with free talks and children's creative sessions, and has the benefit of Lloyd Park being right on its doorstep.

—

Lloyd Park, Forest Road, E17 4PP

www.wmgallery.org.uk

Walthamstow Central tube/rail

Peter Schuyff exhibition, 2020

FIVE COMMERCIAL SPACES

As one of Europe's foremost contemporary art destinations, London is home to at least one venue operated by each of the world's biggest galleristas – many have more than one. Whether purpose-built or sited in carefully converted buildings, these original spaces are great places in which to see what some of the world's biggest names in art are currently working on.

❖ WHITE CUBE MASON'S YARD
CENTRAL LONDON

The enfant terrible of the art world (actually the Eton-educated son of a Tory peer), Jay Jopling made his name and fortune representing the YBAs (Young British Artists) who exploded onto the art scene in the 1990s. His two galleries in London (in Bermondsey and Mayfair) are always worth a visit, but the Mason's Yard one is the easiest to get to.

———

25–26 Mason's Yard, SW1Y 6BU
whitecube.com
Green Park or Piccadilly Circus tube

Michael Craig-Martin exhibition, 2019

✣ GAGOSIAN
CENTRAL LONDON

Designed by Caruso St John, Gagosian's King's Cross gallery is one of the largest and most elegant former garage spaces in town. Large-scale regeneration has changed the area beyond belief in recent years, but its gritty atmosphere remains, giving the gallery a dynamic edge. Expect to see world-class, large-scale sculpture and painting.

—

6–24 Britannia Street, WC1X 9JD
gagosian.com
King's Cross St Pancras tube/rail

Michael Craig-Martin exhibition, 2019

❧ VICTORIA MIRO

NORTH LONDON

Victoria Miro's unusual space at Wharf Road showcases work by the gallerist's forty-strong roster of international artists. Permanent works include *The Seas Leaves...*, a huge neon illumination by Ian Hamilton Finlay. Two additional works by the same artist can be found in the gallery's lush landscaped garden.

---

16 Wharf Road, N1 7RW
www.victoria-miro.com
Old Street tube/rail

Wolfgang Tillmans, The State We're In, A, 2015

❖ NEWPORT STREET GALLERY
SOUTH-EAST LONDON

Damien Hirst's gallery is famously not what you'd expect of the man who likes to put dead animals in tanks and encrust skulls with diamonds. Devoted to displaying works from his personal collection, the six exhibition spaces here are understated but stunning – wittily heightened by Pharmacy 2, Hirst's kaleidoscopic take on a café.

—

Newport Street, SE11 6AJ
www.newportstreetgallery.com
Vauxhall tube/rail

❖ MAUREEN PALEY
EAST LONDON

One of the first gallerists to set up shop in East London (in 1984), Maureen Paley occupied space in Herald Street for more than twenty years. Now located on Three Colts Lane, the gallery hosts artists that include the likes of Turner Prize winners Wolfgang Tillmans, Lawrence Abu Hamdan and Gillian Wearing.

—

60 Three Colts Lane, E2 6GQ
www.maureenpaley.com
Bethnal Green tube

✤ THE WALLACE COLLECTION

CENTRAL LONDON

What a difference a few hundred metres can make. Close to the hustle and bustle of Oxford Street, approaching from Selfridges along Duke Street, elegant little Manchester Square hoves into view with, at its centre, an unlikely looking mansion that was once Sir Richard Wallace's Hertford House. Like the Marquesses of Hertford before him, Wallace was a keen collector of European arts and crafts, and over two centuries the family amassed 5,500 pieces representing some of the world's best examples of fine and decorative art from the fifteenth to the nineteenth centuries. It is, perhaps, the French eighteenth-century works that are the most arresting; paintings, porcelain and furniture snapped up by the wealthy English noblemen during sales held after the French Revolution. Knowing you're admiring pieces that once belonged to French families whose members lost their lives in that revolution adds an emotional dimension to them . . . even more so when you take in the four rooms of arms and armour.

Hertford House, Manchester Square, W1U 3BN
wallacecollection.org
Bond Street tube

Frans Hals, *Laughing Cavalier*, 1624

Sharif Persaud 'Have You Ever Had' exhibition, 2020

Sharif Persaud 'Have You Ever Had' exhibition, 2020

✤ AUTOGRAPH

EAST LONDON

Autograph occupies a modern, luminous space in the creative hub of Shoreditch at the heart of London's East End. Describing itself as dedicated to sharing 'the work of artists who use photography and film to highlight issues of identity, representation, human rights and social justice', the gallery is always a sure bet for an exhibition that will leave you asking questions and wanting to know more about its themes and artists. The focus here is very much on promoting the work of international black and minority ethnic (BAME) artists, and most of the exhibitions feature a wide range of accompanying activities and events aimed at all ages, many of which are free. The building Autograph is housed in, Rivington Place, is well worth a wander too. It was designed by British-Ghanian architect David Adjaye and was the UK's first permanent public space dedicated to diversity in the visual arts.

—

Rivington Place, EC2A 3BA
autograph.org.uk
Old Street tube/rail or Shoreditch High Street overground

✤ SOUTH LONDON GALLERY

SOUTH-EAST LONDON

Set across two sites (the original Victorian gallery and, nearby, what served as Camberwell Fire Station from 1867), South London Gallery has become the London home of the annual show of recent art school graduates, New Contemporaries, curated by a changing panel of established artists. Running for ten weeks at the start of the year, it's an excellent opportunity to gauge current art trends and spot stars of the future. The rest of the time, there's a similar emphasis on new art and emerging talent, and SLG has given many international artists their first solo shows. There's a tasteful café and a small but well-curated bookshop, and free cultural walks relating to exhibition themes are held every month.

—

65–67 Peckham Road, SE5 8UH
www.southlondongallery.org
Peckham Rye overground/rail

'Bloomberg New Contemporaries' exhibition, 2019

National Portrait Gallery

SEVEN MORE, BIG AND SMALL

Camden Arts Centre, NW3

A community-focused space promoting emerging international artists – Kara Walker is among those whose first UK exhibition was held here.
www.camdenartscentre.org
Camden tube

Chisenhale Gallery, E3

An innovative, non-profit contemporary art gallery housed in a former veneer factory and brewery building.
chisenhale.org.uk; Mile End tube

Tate Britain, SW1

British art from 1500 to the twenty-first century; includes the world's largest collection of works by JMW Turner.
tate.org.uk; Pimlico tube

Tate Modern, SE1

A fabulous permanent collection of international modern art in a former power station, with large-scale, site-specific installations in its Turbine Hall.
tate.org.uk; Blackfriars tube/rail

National Gallery, WC2

World-class works from the Middle Ages to the twentieth century; come back again and again to see works by Da Vinci, Caravaggio, Constable, Vermeer, Van Gogh and so many more.
www.nationalgallery.org.uk
Charing Cross tube/rail or Leicester Square tube

National Portrait Gallery, WC2

The world's most extensive collection of sitters (by some of the world's greatest artists) represented in thousands of paintings, photographs, drawings and prints.
www.npg.org.uk; Charing Cross tube/rail or Leicester Square tube

Two Temple Place, WC2

This jaw-dropping neo-Gothic mansion home of William Waldorf Astor holds exhibitions (Jan–Apr) covering everything from the age of jazz in Britain to Sussex Modernism.
twotempleplace.org; Temple tube

5

PERFORMING ARTS

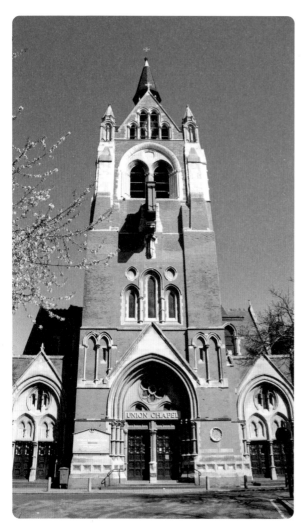

✤ DAYLIGHT MUSIC
NORTH LONDON

The magnificent Union Chapel in Islington is known for gigs as well as philanthropic ventures, and it combines the two in Daylight Music. These sessions take place on occasional Saturday afternoons (noon–2pm), and feature a mixed bag of musicians: singers, bands, soloists and even orchestras have performed. The same bill might hold a heartfelt singer/songwriter and the fabulous London Accordion Orchestra; some are themed (at Christmas, or around the London Jazz Festival). The standard is always high, and part of the pleasure lies in hearing new, unexpected voices. The afternoon runs on a pay-what-you-can basis (the chapel suggests £5 per person, but it really is a suggestion), and it's a very family-friendly occasion, with babies and children welcome. Top tip – if you'd rather avoid toddlers, head to the pews upstairs, where you still get a great view of the stage.

—

Compton Terrace, N1 2UN
www.unionchapel.org.uk
Highbury & Islington tube/rail

⚜ RADIO AND TV SHOWS

<u>VARIOUS LOCATIONS</u>

The BBC offers free tickets to a wide range of its radio and TV shows, and while some are seriously oversubscribed (*Strictly Come Dancing*), many others are more easily accessible. There are tickets for concert recordings, comedy shows, quizzes and political bunfights. Applause Store has tickets for shows across various TV channels, including *Britain's Got Talent* and *A League of Their Own*. *Pointless* and *8 Out of 10 Cats* fans should check out SRO Audiences, while Lost in TV has tickets

for shows such as *Who Wants to be a Millionaire* and *Ninja Warrior UK*. Persevere and sooner or later you will get tickets. Shows are mainly recorded in London or Manchester, but others take place around the country. Once you've got your tickets, bear in mind that there are usually more tickets than seats (to guard against no-shows), so arrive early to be sure of your place.

----

www.bbc.co.uk/showsandtours/shows
www.applausestore.com
www.sroaudiences.com
lostintv.com

Royal Festival Hall

FREE GIGS

You can see free live music most nights of the week across the city's pubs, if you know where to look – and not just in pubs; old churches, arts centres and record stores also host regular gigs. Here are our favourites.

ARTS CENTRES

VARIOUS LOCATIONS

The central foyer space at the South Bank's Royal Festival Hall (*www.southbankcentre.co.uk*) has lunchtime music events every Friday – a good mix of classical, jazz, folk, world music and experimental. In King's Cross, Kings Place's (*www.kingsplace.co.uk*) light-filled foyers and waterside terraces all host regular free events.

Guildhall School concert, Trafalgar Square

COLLEGES AND THEATRES

VARIOUS LOCATIONS

Royal College of Music

For classical music, the Guildhall School (*www.gsmd.ac.uk*), Royal Academy of Music (*www.ram.ac.uk*) and Royal College of Music (*www.rcm.ac.uk*) all host free concerts by students (daytime and evening). And, run by the Barbican, the London Symphony Orchestra's (*lso.co.uk/lso-discovery.html*) Discovery Free Friday Lunchtime Concert series at LSO St Luke's is a great 45-minute introduction to the work of the orchestra. The Royal Opera House's (*roh.org.uk*) Live at Lunch one-hour recitals take place every Friday in the foyer of the Linbury Theatre.

109

House of Vans

RECORD STORES AND BRANDED SPACES

<u>VARIOUS LOCATIONS</u>

One of London's best record stores, Rough Trade East (*roughtrade.com*), regularly hosts free gigs, signings and Q&As by established and up-and-coming artists, while House of Vans (*houseofvanslondon.com*), in Waterloo, puts on a free gig every month as part of its Sessions series, as well as the occasional free gig by surprisingly big names such as the Vaccines.

Rough Trade East

The Finsbury

The Old Blue Last

PUBS

VARIOUS LOCATIONS

The Sebright Arms' (*sebrightarms.com*) monthly Good Karma Club showcases new talent, while The Old Blue Last (*www.theoldbluelast.com*), Shacklewell Arms (*www.shacklewellarms.com*), The Finsbury (*www.thefinsbury.co.uk*) and Waiting Room (*waitingroomn16.com*) all offer reliably enjoyable acts. In Camden and Clapham respectively, The Monarch's (*monarchbar.com*) monthly Animal Farm Hog Roast and free gigs at the Bread and Roses (*breadandrosespub.com*) won't disappoint.

RSA

❖ TALKS AND LECTURES

VARIOUS LOCATIONS

A heartening number of London institutions offer free talks, and Gresham College (*www.gresham. ac.uk*) is a good place to start. The lectures cover a wide range of categories, from film, music and history to law, business and medicine, and the speakers are an impressive bunch. Talks are run on a first-come, first-served basis, apart from a few ticketed (but still free) events. The Royal Society for the Encouragement of Arts, Manufactures and Commerce (RSA; *www.thersa.org*) also has a wide-ranging programme, with a focus on current events; talks are ticketed. Lunchtime talks at the Guildhall Library (*www.cityoflondon.gov. uk/things-to-do/guildhall-library*) are history-focused, while those at the National Gallery (*www. nationalgallery.org.uk*) stick with art; University College London (UCL; *www.ucl.ac.uk/events/ lunch-hour-lectures*) has a Lunch Hour Lecture series showcasing research work at the university – just register to attend. The seriously science-minded should look out for occasional lectures at the Francis Crick Institute (*www.crick.ac.uk*), while techies will appreciate the public lectures in the Department of Computing at Imperial College (*www.imperial.ac.uk/computing*).

Francis Crick Institute

⚜ OLD BAILEY TRIALS

THE CITY

Watching a live trial offers a fascinating glimpse into the British judicial process, and doing so in the storied spaces of the Central Criminal Court of England and Wales (known as the Old Bailey after the street on which it stands) particularly so. Part of it occupies the site of the medieval Newgate gaol, and public hangings took place in the street outside until 1868, but it's the wood-panelled courtrooms within that evoke this institution's more recent history, in which the likes of Dr Crippen, the Kray Twins, Jeremy Thorpe and the Yorkshire Ripper were all tried. Aim for courts 1 and 2 if you want to feel their dark shadows, but be prepared to queue. Or opt, instead, for the other old building courtrooms (nos. 3, 4, 17 and 18) or one of the courts in the new building. Security measures are strict, so bring photo ID but leave mobile phones, cameras, food, drink and writing materials at home – they are all banned.

—

Old Bailey, EC4M 7EH
courttribunalfinder.service.gov.uk/courts/
central-criminal-court
St Paul's tube

✛ CHURCH CONCERTS

<u>VARIOUS LOCATIONS</u>

Daytime recitals of amazingly good music can be found in churches all over London, but they're concentrated in the centre, particularly in the City. All those listed here are free, but note that often there's a suggested donation or collection. City churches St Stephen Walbrook, St Bartholomew the Great, St Bride's, St Olaf, St Mary-le-Bow, St Michael Cornhill and St Lawrence Jewry and more (*www.london-city-churches. org.uk*) hold regular recitals. Elsewhere, St James's Piccadilly (*www.sjp.org.uk*) has lunchtime concerts on Monday, Wednesday and Friday, while St Martin-in-the-Fields (*www.stmartin-in-the-fields.org*) holds them on Monday, Tuesday and Friday. Organ recitals can be heard on Monday lunchtimes at Southwark Cathedral (*cathedral. southwark.anglican.org*), and on Sundays at 4.45pm at Westminster Cathedral (*www.westminstercathedral. org.uk*) – these two cathedrals do not have an entrance fee.

St Michael Cornhill

Electric Pedals

BST Hyde Park

❖ OUTDOOR FILM SCREENINGS

VARIOUS LOCATIONS

During the summer months, many of London's outdoor spaces come alive with the sound of cinema. One of the best is at Scoop (*More London, SE1 2AA, London Bridge tube/rail*), a 1,000-seat amphitheatre that hosts a mix of classic, cult and current movies every week during summer. London parks get in on the action too, with Hyde Park hosting free screenings during the BST Hyde Park music festival (*www.bst-hydepark. com, Marble Arch or Hyde Park Corner tube*), and Victoria Park doing the same during All Points East (*www.allpointseastfestival.com, Bethnal Green tube*). Want to exercise while taking in a movie? The Southbank Centre's Royal Festival Hall riverside terrace (*Belvedere Road, SE1 8XX, www.southbankcentre.co.uk, Waterloo tube/rail*) has weekly free pedal-powered screenings in July and August — and as they're presented by Electric Pedals, hopefully the movie won't run out of steam if you do. West Londoners can head to Wembley Park, where Arena Square unfolds the deckchairs for a Summer on Screen programme (*www. wembleypark.com/summer-on-screen-programme, Wembley Park tube*), including Hollywood hits, singalongs and Bollywood blockbusters.

Totally Thames

FIVE FREE FESTIVALS

Pride in London
London's LGBT+ community marches loud and proud on its colourful Pride in London Parade through the streets of central London each June, with lots of free activities and performances in and around Trafalgar Square.
prideinlondon.org

Eid in the Square, WC2
More than 25,000 Londoners come together the Saturday after Eid al-Fitr to enjoy family-friendly activities, live music, food stalls and more in Trafalgar Square in this celebration of Ramadan's month of fasting.
www.london.gov.uk/events
Charing Cross tube/rail

Totally Thames
The consistently creative and diverse programme of each September's Totally Thames festival makes it a winner for lovers of culture and art, with pop-up performances, boating events, art installations, river clean-ups, live performances, talks, workshops and more.
totallythames.org

Pearly Kings and Queens Harvest Festival, EC2
This traditional harvest festival is held on the last Sunday afternoon in September at Guildhall Yard. It not only brings together Pearly Kings and Queens from all over London, but also features traditional activities such as Morris and maypole dancing and performances from marching bands.
www.pearlysociety.co.uk
Bank tube

Lambeth Country Show, SE24
Food stalls, live music, animal displays and crafts stalls are just some of the things to enjoy at July's Lambeth Country Show in Brockwell Park . . . as well as prize-winning pets, vegetables, flowers and produce.
lambethcountryshow.co.uk, Herne Hill, North Dulwich or Tulse Hill rail

6

BUILDINGS AND BUILT SPACES

✜ SOUTHBANK CENTRE

CENTRAL LONDON

Built, in part, as the centrepiece of the Festival of Britain and spanning two distinct styles – the sleek lines of 1950s modernism and concrete brutalism of the 1970s – the Southbank Centre is a jewel in the crown of London's cultural scene. The Royal Festival Hall completed for the festival was joined almost two decades later by the Queen Elizabeth Hall, Purcell Room and Hayward Gallery to create an art space and riverside terrace that offer lots to enjoy, particularly if you like modern architecture. Look up above the central bar of the Festival Hall, maybe while taking in a free concert, and you'll realise how similar the space is to a cruise ship – a deliberate design element. And while you're listening to surprisingly good buskers on the river path or admiring the skill of the skateboarders under Waterloo Bridge, take time to appreciate the forest of octagonal mushroom columns and textures of the stairways and walkways – all formed in concrete using timber casts.

Belvedere Road, SE1 8XX
www.southbankcentre.co.uk
Waterloo tube/rail

✤ THE CHARTERHOUSE
THE CITY

What a storied past this 600-year-old site has. It begins as a burial site for more than 50,000 victims of the Black Death before becoming a fourteenth-century Carthusian monastery torn apart by King Henry VIII (who also tore apart many of those monks who refused to reform during the dissolution of the monasteries). Then, as a private home in a Tudor mansion, it was frequented by both Elizabeth I and James I, before being purchased in 1611 by Thomas Sutton, who established an almshouse here, and subsequently a school for poor children that went on to become the famous Charterhouse public school, now in Surrey. Today, The Charterhouse functions as a supported living complex and care home for socially and financially challenged men and, since 2017, women. A small but interesting museum, chapel, grounds and garden are all free, as are occasional events, including concerts in the chapel and weekly ten-minute tales on Wednesday lunchtimes.

—

Charterhouse Square, EC1M 6AN
www.thecharterhouse.org
Barbican tube or Farringdon tube/rail

✣ LONGPLAYER INSTALLATION
EAST LONDON

London's only lighthouse is found at Trinity Buoy Wharf, in Docklands. It houses the Longplayer Tibetan 'singing bowls' installation. Jem Finer's musical composition is set to run for 1,000 years: it began on 31 December 1999 and should continue without repetition until the last second of 2999; then it begins all over again. Climb to the top of the lighthouse for views over the Thames and Docklands, but note that Trinity Buoy Wharf is open on Saturdays and Sundays only. Also on the wharf are various art installations, and an ex-docker's hut converted into a small museum dedicated to scientist Michael Faraday.

—

64 Orchard Place, E14 0JW

www.trinitybuoywharf.com

Canning Town tube

❧ GREENWICH FOOT TUNNEL

<u>SOUTH-EAST LONDON</u>

This engineering marvel, opened in 1902, is fun whether you're five or fifty. There's the thrill of being under the river, the echoing nature of the tile-lined interior, and the magical feeling of descending on one side of London and popping up on another. The sense of dislocation is helped by the fact that Island Gardens on the north bank and Greenwich to the south are very different in character. There are lifts at either end, or you can take the stairs: eighty-seven steps at Island Gardens, one hundred in Greenwich.

—

www.royalgreenwich.gov.uk/info/200259/transport_and_travel/893/foot_tunnels
Cutty Sark or Island Gardens DLR

✤ ALL SAINTS, MARGARET STREET

<u>CENTRAL LONDON</u>

There are many reasons why All Saints has been hailed as 'a pioneering building of the High Victorian Gothic', a style typical of British architecture from the 1850s to the 1870s, and there are just as many reasons why it's worth a visit. Designed by William Butterfield, the church sits neatly within a small three-sided front courtyard, buttressed by the vicarage on one side and what was the choir school on the other, all of which combine to emphasise its height and grandeur. The most striking feature of its exterior is the innovative use of red brick, patterned with black brick and inset stone decoration, a delightful departure from the grey sandstone typical of Gothic Revival churches of the 1840s. But even this level of decoration barely prepares you for the richness of an interior where nothing has been left undecorated, from the stained-glass windows and the painted frieze tiles to the walls and ceiling.

—

7 Margaret Street, W1W 8JG
www.allsaintsmargaretstreet.org.uk
Oxford Circus tube

✥ BAPS SHRI SWAMINARAYAN MANDIR
NORTH LONDON

Popularly known as the 'Neasden Temple', the Mandir is a traditional place of Hindu worship and the most striking building for miles around. The materials that make the temple (Bulgarian limestone, Italian and Indian marble) were carved and coded in India, and then transported to London to be assembled; it opened in 1995. As well as being a holy building – services are held daily – community outreach is also important, and visitors are welcome. Guests enter through the *haveli* – a cultural centre with a prayer hall, classrooms and a souvenir shop; it's an airy wooden building with intricate carved motifs on what seems like every surface. In contrast, the temple is full of bright, white marble, spectacular carvings and colourful shrines to deities of the Hindu faith. Do read the guidelines before a tour: modest dress is required, shoes have to be removed, and no photos are allowed inside the building.

—

105–119 Brentfield Road, NW10 8LD
londonmandir.baps.org
206 or 224 bus

✢ HOUSES OF PARLIAMENT

CENTRAL LONDON

Anyone with a British passport can visit the Houses of Parliament for free. Simply by emailing your MP or a member of the House of Lords, you'll be able to take a seventy-five-minute tour of various parts of the building – often including Westminster Hall, Central Lobby, St Stephen's Hall and, if they're not in session, one or both chambers – with a guide who'll entertainingly relay information about how both houses work, as well as give you fascinating tidbits about their traditions and historical highlights. If that all sounds so enticing that you don't want to wait the few weeks it usually takes to get a booking, last-minute tours are often available too, by emailing visitparliament@parliament.uk.

Palace of Westminster, SW1A 0AA
www.parliament.uk/visiting
Westminster tube

St Stephen Walbrook

CITY OF LONDON CHURCHES

The churches in the Square Mile offer a beguiling mix of history, architecture and art, not to mention excellent coffee, all within an easily walkable area. Some have origins as far back as the eleventh century; famous figures have worshipped and worked in them; most have been destroyed and rebuilt, often more than once. Several of the churches have a strong musical heritage, and listening to a choir or an organ recital, in concert or during a service, is something to be cherished. You may also hear a peal of bells – usually at weekends, as these marathon sessions can last for hours. (*To investigate further, see www.london-city-churches.org.uk, the website of the architectural heritage charity Friends of City Churches.*)

✣ ST STEPHEN WALBROOK

Designed by Sir Christopher Wren, St Stephen
Walbrook had to be partially rebuilt after bomb
damage during World War II, but it remains a
handsome church, with a beautiful dome. The
open interior holds a striking marble altar by
Henry Moore, surrounded by a brightly coloured
kneeler designed by Patrick Heron. The
Samaritans began here: vicar Chad Varah
started the organisation in 1953.

---

39 Walbrook, EC4N 8BN
ststephenwalbrook.net
Bank tube

✣ ST MARY WOOLNOTH

This imposing early-eighteenth-century church
is the only one by Nicholas Hawksmoor in
the Square Mile. He also designed some of the
furnishings, including the reredos and a striking
pulpit. Another claim to fame – the church is
mentioned in TS Eliot's 'The Waste Land'. There's
a busy coffee stall in the porch, but once inside
the main building, the atmosphere is solemn
and the twenty-first century slips away.

Lombard Street, EC3V 9EA
stml.org.uk
Bank tube

St Mary Woolnoth

✤ ST MARY-LE-BOW

Rebuilt by Sir Christopher Wren after the Great Fire of London in 1666, and damaged again in 1941, this is the home of the famous 'Bow Bells', one of the few sets of twelve bells in the City – you can call yourself a Cockney if you were born within hearing distance of them. The church has a spacious crypt – now used as a café – and a set of modern stained-glass windows, by John Hayward.

Cheapside, EC2V 6AU
www.stmarylebow.org.uk
Mansion House tube

✤ ST BARTHOLOMEW THE GREAT

Come to evensong at St Bartholomew, when you can hear the impressive choir and appreciate the historic, Grade I listed surroundings. Either that, or attend a lunchtime concert – otherwise, outside church services, there's a charge to visit. As well as the architecture, there are several notable works of art on display, of which Damien Hirst's gilded *Exquisite Pain* is the most obvious.

West Smithfield, EC1A 9DS
www.greatstbarts.com
Barbican tube

✣ ST DUNSTAN IN THE EAST

St Dunstan in the East is an interesting example of a church that wasn't restored after the 1941 Blitz during World War II. Instead, the elegant ruins of the twelfth-century church (Grade I listed) now surround a small, peaceful garden. It's overlooked by the tower and steeple (by Sir Christopher Wren), which survived the bombing.

St Dunstan's Hill, EC3R 5DD
Fenchurch Street rail

✣ ST MARY ABCHURCH

The crowning glory of stately St Mary Abchurch is the painted dome, designed by Sir Christopher Wren and decorated by William Snow, a parishioner. The reredos, carved by Grinling Gibbons, runs it a close second. The church was completed to Wren's design in 1686, and much remains from that time, including the original high pews and a mighty wooden pulpit.

Abchurch Lane, EC4N 7BA
Cannon Street tube/rail

❖ OPEN HOUSE LONDON

<u>VARIOUS LOCATIONS</u>

For one weekend a year (in mid-September), there's a golden opportunity to venture inside hundreds of London's buildings, many of which are normally closed to the public. Since the project started, in 1992, Open House has grown to include more than 800 buildings, ranging from architect-designed private homes and tiny Calvinist chapels to London's last grand music hall, Wilton's, and big-hitters such as the BT Tower and the Foreign & Commonwealth Office. Some of the most interesting buildings aren't in the centre of town – for example, the Baitul Futuh Mosque in Morden, the brutalist landmark Balfron Tower in Poplar, and the Blue House Yard, an innovative regeneration project in Wood Green. There are associated free walks and talks, too – it's the perfect excuse to get to know London better.

—

openhouselondon.org.uk

BT Tower

✤ BARBICAN CENTRE

THE CITY

The Barbican Centre makes a great rainy-day excursion, as the covered walkways and interior activities make it enjoyable in all weathers. The library is worth a visit: there's a children's library, and a floor devoted to music, which always has interesting music-related exhibitions. The Curve gallery hosts specially commissioned installations and soundscapes, while there are regular free live music events in the foyer. The Barbican Conservatory is good for a blast of heat and colour – though opening times are restricted, so check before you go. Around 2,000 species of plants and trees are growing inside the giant hothouse, from a variety of terrains and ranging from towering trees to flowering cacti. If you're lucky with the weather, head for the lakeside terraces and admire the brutal architecture.

—

Silk Street, EC2Y 8DS
www.barbican.org.uk
Barbican tube or Moorgate tube/rail

Greenwich Park

LONDON'S BEST VIEWS

Alexandra Palace, N22
Panoramic views of the city from one of the highest spots in North London.

Alexandra Palace rail

Greenwich Park, SE10
Climb the hill for an amazing wide-open vista, with the National Maritime Museum and the Royal Naval College in the foreground and, across the river, Docklands.

Cutty Sark DLR or Maze Hill rail

King Henry's Mound, TW10
Richmond Park's protected view – from a Bronze-age barrow – of St Paul's Cathedral.

Richmond tube/overground/rail

Nunhead Cemetery, SE15
Another classic view of St Paul's, this time from an atmospheric, overgrown cemetery.

Nunhead rail

One New Change, EC4M 9AF
Take the lift to the top of this Jean Nouvel-designed shopping centre for impressive close-up views of the City.

St Paul's tube

Sky Garden, EC3M 8AF
Enjoy the indoor garden and the open-air terrace at the top of the Walkie Talkie. It's free, but you need to book a slot (*skygarden.london*).

Monument tube

Parliament Hill, NW3
This breezy Hampstead Heath highpoint has views out over central London and beyond.

Gospel Oak or Hampstead Heath overground

7

SEASONAL
LONDON

✢ GREENWICH+DOCKLANDS INTERNATIONAL FESTIVAL

<u>SOUTH-EAST LONDON</u>

Don't miss this annual festival of outdoor performance – it's a blast. Past productions have covered theatre, dance, circus, street arts and installation, in spaces as diverse as Guildhall Yard, the Old Royal Naval College and Eltham High Street. Expect immersive events, fireworks, light shows, spectacle and giant puppets: one previous show, *Moby Dick*, saw a massive whale built and dismantled by hand amid dancing and circus skills; another, *MO and the Red Ribbon*, was a promenade performance through the streets of Bow, following a giant child puppet. GDIF runs for around three weeks at the end of June, beginning of July; many of the performances are family-friendly, and there are opportunities to volunteer as well as spectate.

festival.org/gdif

✤ OPEN AIR THEATRE SEASON AT SCOOP

<u>CENTRAL LONDON</u>

Many London parks offer outdoor theatre seasons during the summer months, but none are free – with the notable exception of the annual Free Open Air Theatre Season at Scoop. Running during August in a 1,000-seater purpose-built amphitheatre on the banks of the River Thames, the plays performed here are an eclectic and bold mix of highbrow to eyebrow-raising, spanning the gamut from child-friendly and family shows such as *The Jungle Book* and *The Adventures of* *Jason and the Argonauts* to a rock musical based on *Crime and Punishment*, via Wagner's Ring Cycle plays, Greek tragedies and, of course, Shakespeare. The season has run every year since 2003, thanks to the enthusiasm and commitment of its founder Phil Willmott, and its laudable aim of making classic texts and new work accessible and enjoyable to all, while also offering opportunities to diverse directors, actors and other theatrical creatives, is to be celebrated. Bravo, we say!

—

Queen's Walk, More London, SE1 2DB

www.freeopenairtheatre.org

London Bridge tube/rail

✣ CITY CEREMONIES

THE CITY

Of the many quaint and picturesque ceremonies that take place in the City of London, Cart Marking is a particular treat. An old form of licensing, these days the tradition sees vintage lorries, veteran motorcycles, horse-drawn carts, retro delivery vans and a few modern vehicles attend the Guildhall Yard to be branded with a red-hot iron by dignitaries including the Lord Mayor. The vehicles await their turn in the streets around Guildhall (position yourself on Gresham Street for a prime view). The ceremony takes place in July. An even odder affair is the Sheep Drive over London Bridge, organised by the Worshipful Company of Woolmen every September; it's now a charitable event in which you can buy tickets to be part of a sheep drive (*sheepdrive. london*). For more processions, ceremonies and costumed traditions, see the City of London website (*www. cityoflondon.gov.uk*).

Receiver, Huma Bhabha, 2019

❖ FRIEZE OUTDOOR SCULPTURE

NORTH LONDON

Each summer, Regent's Park is transformed into an Instagrammer's paradise with the annual arrival of twenty-five pieces of outdoor art; yes, Frieze Sculpture has come to town. Frieze proper runs for a weekend in October and is geared to the serious and commercially minded art lover. Meanwhile, its egalitarian sibling can be found in the southernmost reaches of the park from July to early October, delighting park users who come to relax, eat their lunchtime sandwiches or do a double take as they jog by. The emphasis is on the playful yet insightful – a full-size reproduction of a 1973 Jaguar E-Type Matchbox toy car complete with dents and chipped paint by Brazilian artist Vik Muniz is a typical example. Works by well-established stars, such as Tracey Emin, rub shoulders with emerging talent, and with a selection policy encompassing the humorous, political and downright fun, it's an enjoyable experience whether you're into art or not.

—

Regent's Park, NW1 4LL

frieze.com/tags/frieze-sculpture

Regent's Park tube

Final Days, Kaws, 2017

Stroke, Tony Cragg, 2017

✤ PANORAMA PRACTICE
WEST LONDON

Integral to the Notting Hill Carnival since it began in 1966 is steel pan, the sound of the Caribbean that originated with musicians adapting oil drums into surprisingly versatile instruments in 1930s Trinidad. On the Saturday evening of the carnival, head to Notting Hill for the National Panorama Steel Band Competition, where the country's best steel pan bands showcase their skills. It is held from around 7pm at Emslie Horniman's Pleasance Park.

The event isn't free, but go a couple of hours earlier and walk around the surrounding streets, and you'll find all eight contesting finalists doing full rehearsals of their numbers, far away enough from each other that their sounds are distinct. You can get really close to the bands and even individual pannists, food stalls are on hand, drink is BYO, and the atmosphere is lively and lovely.

———

Emslie Horniman's Pleasance Park, W10 3DH
nhcarnival.org/saturday
Westbourne Park tube

❖ GREAT RIVER RACE

VARIOUS LOCATIONS

The organisers describe this fabulous parade of boats as 'London's River Marathon', with more than 300 vessels racing from Millwall to Ham (34.7 km/21.6 miles), powered by oars or paddles only. Crews come from all over the world; some are out to win, others compete for charity, or just the fun of it. The sheer variety of boats involved makes spectating interesting, with everything from canoes and skiffs to Chinese dragon boats and Cornish gigs sailing past. Grab a spot along the route – Tower Bridge is a good bet – and watch the teams of sea scouts, Thames watermen and amateur enthusiasts battle it out. The Great River Race is held annually on a Saturday in September – check the website for details.

—

www.greatriverrace.co.uk

✤ LONDON DESIGN FESTIVAL
<u>VARIOUS LOCATIONS</u>

You know when the London Design Festival comes to town because strange structures and activities begin to spring up as far afield as South Kensington and Clerkenwell. It might be a giant undulating bench formed of scaffolding planks, Audi robots creating calligraphy from visitors' text messages, a gigantic Swarovski crystal lens in St Paul's Cathedral or a collection of buildings in Trafalgar Square, but it is always arresting, thoughtful and thought provoking. Begun back in 2003 as a means of promoting and celebrating London's creative industries with exhibitions and events, the festival is now huge, and huge fun, taking in design districts and design routes (clusters of events in one small area or within walking distance of each other), as well as Landmark Projects (major installations by both world-renowned creatives and exciting new talents). Regular events take place in and around the V&A Museum, and are bolstered by occasional special projects – among them, in 2006, a Tom Dixon Chair Grab which saw near-riots when 500 polystyrene chairs by the designer were given away in Trafalgar Square.

—

www.londondesignfestival.com

SEASONAL HIGHLIGHTS

As one of the world's most vibrant cities, London is constantly busy with ceremonies and festivals, and there's creativity everywhere. Events and happenings take place in galleries, museums and parks, as well as on the river and in the streets. The choice ranges from age-old traditions to up-to-the-minute visual spectaculars and exciting sporting contests – there really is something to please everyone.

❖ CHINESE NEW YEAR

CENTRAL LONDON

Centred in Chinatown and spilling into the surrounding West End streets, this vibrant festival takes place in January/February to mark the turn of the lunar year. Catch the parade – complete with dragon dancers – as it passes through on the nearest Sunday to Chinese New Year.

—

chinatown.co.uk

❖ LONDON MARATHON

VARIOUS LOCATIONS

A Sunday in mid-April sees around 36,000 runners competing in the London Marathon, many of them in crazy costumes. The route starts in Greenwich Park and ends in the Mall, with plenty of great vantage points along the way.

---

www.virginmoneylondonmarathon.com

❖ STATE OPENING OF PARLIAMENT

CENTRAL LONDON

The formal beginning of the parliamentary year takes place in May/June and is marked in style by the queen, who travels to the Palace of Westminster in the state coach, accompanied by the Household Cavalry.

---

www.parliament.uk/stateopening

✤ TROOPING THE COLOUR

CENTRAL LONDON

To celebrate her official birthday in June each year, the queen rides in a carriage from Buckingham Palace to Horse Guards Parade, inspects her soldiers, and returns for a flypast. To watch the pageantry without the crowds, catch a Trooping minus the queen, one or two weeks beforehand.

—

www.householddivision.org.uk

✤ NOTTING HILL CARNIVAL

WEST LONDON

Europe's biggest street party takes place over the Sunday and Monday of the August bank holiday weekend, with everything from sound systems and steel bands to parades and Caribbean food stalls. Sunday is the most family-friendly day.

—

www.thelondonnottinghillcarnival.com

✤ CHRISTMAS LIGHTS & WINDOWS

CENTRAL LONDON

The most inventive Christmas lights can be seen
on Carnaby Street, on and around Bond Street
and at Covent Garden Piazza from late November.
For the prettiest windows, see Fortnum & Mason,
Liberty and Selfridges.

❖ LORD MAYOR'S SHOW
<u>THE CITY</u>

This family-friendly spectacle marks the new Lord Mayor's first full day in office, with a procession kicking off at 11am. Horse-drawn carriages, giant inflatables, brass marching bands, military vehicles, heritage buses, Chinese dragons and more join the traditional 100 or so floats. The atmosphere is lively, but it's not too crowded, and it's easy to find a good vantage point. The hour-long procession goes from Mansion House to the Royal Courts of Justice (the return leg leaves Temple just after 1pm and travels along the Embankment and Queen Victoria Street).

In addition, there's a slightly incongruous funfair just outside St Paul's Cathedral and 'festival' areas (food stalls, face painting, music and so on) at Paternoster Square and Bloomberg Arcade, plus guided walks later in the afternoon. A further bonus – the cathedral is free to visit on the day of the show. And because most of the roads along and around the route are closed to traffic, it's a blissfully car-free day too.

lordmayorsshow.london

✤ CHANGING THE GUARD

CENTRAL LONDON

An impressive display with regimental bands playing stirring music, this ceremonial tradition starts at Wellington Barracks where one of the splendidly attired regiments (usually the Foot Guards – Grenadier, Coldstream, Scots, Irish, Welsh) assembles from 10.45am (daily in summer, otherwise check the website for details). The soldiers march the short distance to Buckingham Palace for the forty-five-minute Changing the Guard ceremony, during which the band plays a winning mix of popular and traditional tunes.

———

Buckingham Palace, SW1A 1AA

www.royal.uk/changing-guard

St James's Park tube

BEST OF BONFIRE NIGHT

Coram's Fields, WC1

As you'd expect from a child-exclusive park, Coram's Fields' firework display is very family friendly, starting earlier than the others (usually 6pm) and geared to little ears. Premium-viewing-zone tickets fund Coram's work with children.

Russell Square tube

Wembley Park, HA9

Visitors to this popular event were treated to a mechanical elephant in 2018. In 2019, lantern parades and giant puppets supplemented the firework display as Bonfire Night was combined with Diwali celebrations.

Wembley Park tube

Blackheath, SE3

London's biggest free firework display doesn't just offer very big bangs for no bucks, it supplements it with a day of activities, including a funfair and food stalls from 5pm.

Blackheath rail

Royal Docks Newham, E16

Organised by Newham Council in partnership with the Royal Docks Team, this display's industrial landscape of Millennium Mills makes it great for those Instagram pics, and usually includes a funfair, DJ and food and drink stalls.

Pontoon Dock DLR

Victoria Park, E3

Tower Hamlets' themed displays with music and performative elements never disappoint. And with stalls, live acts and activities for young ones, it's a family-friendly affair.

Bethnal Green or Mile End tube

Waltham Forest, E17

Mulled wine, DJs, a funfair and a fine display (in 2019, set to music curated by DJ Mighty Atom) encapsulate what a firework night should be for – a local community getting together to enjoy its council putting on a great free show.

Walthamstow Central tube

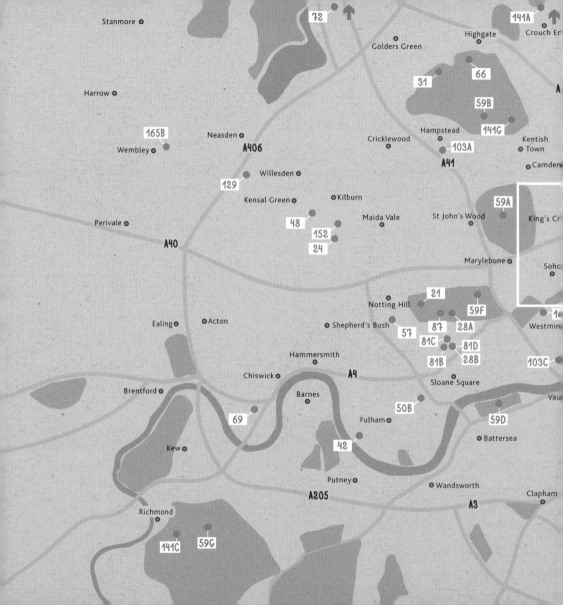

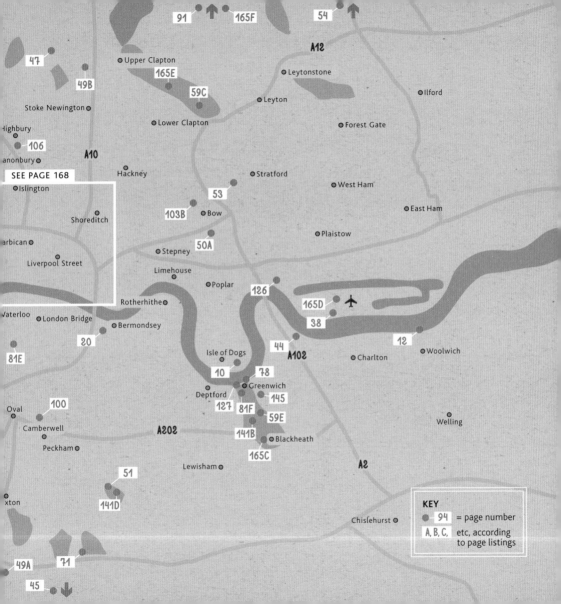

LISTINGS BY AREA

Central London

The City

North London

INDEX

PICTURE CREDITS

Image captions: p1 King Henry's Mound; p2 Pride in London; p4 Mudchute City Farm; p7 South Bank; p8 Portobello Market; p36 Greenwich Park; p60 Horniman Museum and Gardens; p120 Sky Garden; p176 Pearly Kings and Queens.

27L, 53, 77, 129, 150, 151T, 151B; escapetheofficejob/ Alamy Stock Photo: 36; Daniel Finlay/agefotostock: 31; The Finsbury: 110T, 111L; tony french/Alamy Stock Photo: 67; Copyright Fulham Palace: 42, 43; Gareth Gardner: 62, 63TL, 63TR, 63BL, 63BR; Nadiia Gerbish/Shutterstock.com: 140; giorgiogalano/iStock.com: 8; Courtesy of Good Gym: 18; Sandor Gora/Shutterstock.com: 28; Courtesy of Guildhall Art Gallery: 90; Gwoeii/Shutterstock.com: 127B; Steve Heap/Shutterstock.com: 12; hipproductions/Shutterstock. com: 21; Horniman Museum and Gardens: 70T; Peter Horree/Alamy Stock Photo: 24; I Wei Huang: 112; I Wei Huang/ Shutterstock.com: 22, 47, 135L; Richard I'Anson: 154; IR_ Stone/iStock: 17; Jeffrey Isaac Greenberg 5+/Alamy Stock Photo: 26; JBLumix/iStock: 55; jean.cuomo/Shutterstock. com: 127T; JMA Photography: 118; JuliaST/Shutterstock. com: 20; Dinko G Kyuchukov/Shutterstock.com: 56B Chris Lawrence/Alamy Stock Photo: 41; lazyllama/Shutterstock. com: 157R; Mariia Levochkina/Shutterstock.com: 134L; Dirk Lindner: 124; Courtey of London Mithraeum Bloomberg SPACE: 68; M.Sobreira/Alamy Stock Photo: 138B; dov makabaw/Alamy Stock Photo: 30; Bruno Mameli/Shutterstock.com: 69; mauritius images GmbH/Alamy Stock Photo: 115, 147; Zoë Maxwell: 98T, 98B, 99; Mark Mercer: 125; Andrew Michael/Alamy Stock Photo: 56T; mikecphoto/ Shutterstock.com: 136, 159T; miscellany/Alamy Stock Photo: 132; monkeybusinessimages/Getty Images: 138T; Susan Montgomery/Alamy Stock Photo: 108; nobleIMAGES/Alamy Stock Photo: 54; Nathaniel Noir/Alamy Stock Photo: 139; Tom Oldham/Shutterstock: 158R; Courtesy of Our Parks: 16; oversnap/iStock: 33T; PA Images/Alamy Stock Photo: 109T; Padmayogini/Shutterstock.com: 148T, 148B, 157L, 159B, 176; Pajor Pawel/Shutterstock.com: 120; mark phillips/Alamy Stock Photo: 51L; Photographers Gallery: 88, 89; pio3/Shutterstock.com: 109B; Isabelle

Plasschaert/Alamy Stock Photo: 4; Larry Platner/Shutterstock.com: 48; Queen's House: 78T, 78B, 79; r.nagy/ Shutterstock.com: 131; Courtesy of the RAF Museum: 72, 73L, 73T, 73B; Becan Rickard-Elliot: 117L; robertharding/ Alamy Stock Photo: 130; Lorna Roberts/Shutterstock.com: 158L; Roccooiud/Shutterstock.com: 50B; Angeles Rodenas/ Alamy Stock Photo: 152, 153; Marcin Rogozinski/Alamy Stock Photo: 44; GRANT ROONEY PREMIUM/Alamy Stock Photo: 122, 149; Rory James: 117R; Marco Saracco/ Alamy Stock Photo: 40; © Science Museum Group: 80; seancooneyfoto/Shutterstock.com: 163; Alex Segre/Alamy Stock Photo: 58; galit seligmann/Alamy Stock Photo: 39; Courtesy of Serpentine Gallery: 86, 87; Joe Shlabotnik: 14; Felix Shoughi/Alamy Stock Photo: 55B; Doug Southall for GDIF 2015: 145; Sophia Spring/Horniman Museum and Gardens: 60; 70B Andy Stagg: 100, 101T, 101B; Sterling Images/Shutterstock.com: 123; IR Stone/Shutterstock.com: 38; Edmund Sumner-VIEW/Alamy Stock Photo: 142; Phil Swallow/Shutterstock.com: 160; Sandor Szmutko/Shutterstock.com: 161; Murat Taner/Getty Images: 66; Megan Taylor / Horniman Museum and Gardens: 71; © The artist. Photo © White Cube (Theo Christelis): 92; © Wolfgang Tillmans, courtesy Maureen Paley, London / Hove: 95R; Courtesy of Totally Thames: 104; tottoto/Shutterstock. com: 50T, 51R; tric83/iStock: 33B; Pat Tuson/Alamy Stock Photo: 106; Alena Veasey/Shutterstock.com: 111R; Kiev. Victor/Shutterstock.com: 29T; VictorHuang/Getty Images: 46, 84; © Victoria Miro: 94; © The Trustees of the Wallace Collection: 96T, 96B, 97; Warren King for GDIF 2016: 144; Cedric Weber/Shutterstock.com: 19; Wellcome Collection 2019: 64, 65L, 65R; Monica Wells/Alamy Stock Photo: 156; WENN Rights Ltd / Alamy Stock Photo : 110B; © James Whitaker: 126; Wikipedia: 45, 137B; Willy Barton/Shutterstock.com: 25; Courtesy of Wilton's: 137T.

First published in 2021 by Frances Lincoln Publishing,
an imprint of The Quarto Group.
The Old Brewery, 6 Blundell Street
London, N7 9BH,
United Kingdom
T (0)20 7700 6700 .
www.QuartoKnows.com

MIX
Paper from
responsible sources
FSC® C008047